"The Anti-Affiliate Marketing Affiliate Marketing Club" Guide

"THE ANTI-AFFILIATE MARKETING AFFILIATE MARKETING CLUB" GUIDE

Copyright © 2023

Unconventional Insights, Real Results

Welcome to the Anti-Affiliate Marketing Affiliate Marketing Club, where we debunk the traditional, cut through the noise, and reveal the strategies that truly matter. This guide isn't your typical affiliate marketing resource. It's a no-nonsense, action-oriented roadmap that empowers you to launch your affiliate marketing journey, backed by extensive research and unconventional insights.

CONTENTS

INTRODUCTION

Unleash Your Potential

Welcome, champions of the digital world, to a journey like no other. This is not your typical affiliate marketing guide, and I am not your typical narrator. I'm here to ignite the fire within you, to set your aspirations free, and to guide you on a path that breaks away from the ordinary.

In a world filled with promises, buzzwords, and empty claims, we stand apart. We are the Anti Affiliate Marketing Affiliate Marketing Club, and we bring you the no-fluff, no-nonsense guide to success in the digital realm.

But first, let me tell you what makes us different. It's not just about marketing products; it's about marketing yourself. It's about finding your voice in the cacophony of digital noise. It's about sculpting your unique identity in a crowded market. It's about transforming your dreams into tangible, real-life success stories.

In this guide, we won't just feed you information; we'll ignite your determination. We won't just share strategies; we'll fuel your inspiration. We won't just tell you how to start; we'll motivate you to take that first step and the many steps that follow.

Affiliate marketing isn't a path to quick riches; it's a journey to sustainable prosperity. It's not about cutting corners; it's about setting new standards. It's not about blending in; it's about standing out.

Throughout these pages, you'll discover a treasure trove of insights gathered from extensive research, unconventional viewpoints, and real-world successes. We've pored over the competition, dissected their methods, and distilled what truly works. Our mission is to equip you with the knowledge, courage, and drive to defy the odds and emerge as a digital champion.

Are you ready to redefine affiliate marketing? To break free from the herd and create your own path? To shatter the illusions and realize your dreams? Then, my friend, you're in the right place. The journey begins here, and the destination is your vision of success.

Prepare to be inspired, motivated, and equipped with the tools and strategies to make your digital dreams a reality. The Anti Affiliate Marketing Affiliate Marketing Club is not just a guide; it's your ally in the digital marketing revolution. Together, let's break the mold, write our own rules, and become the marketers the world has been waiting for. Your adventure starts now.

CHAPTER ONE

Redefining Affiliate Marketing

Welcome to the first chapter of your transformation, the gateway to redefining affiliate marketing. We're here to revolutionize your perspective on affiliate marketing and set you on a course that breaks the mold.

Traditionally, affiliate marketing has been viewed as a mere revenue stream. But we dare to dream bigger. It's not just about making money; it's about making a mark. It's about breaking free from the conventional and creating a legacy in the digital landscape.

In our club, affiliate marketing isn't a mundane task; it's an art form. It's your canvas, and you are the artist. It's your arena, and you are the gladiator. It's your stage, and you are the performer. It's not about following the footsteps of others; it's about blazing your trail.

Here's the secret: You have the power to shape the narrative. You can redefine what it means to be an affiliate marketer. You can be the pioneer who sets new standards, who transforms the industry. But to do that, you must shed the conventional notions and embrace a new mindset.

Affiliate marketing is more than transactions; it's about transformation. It's about impacting lives, offering solutions, and solving problems. It's about understanding your audience, connecting with them, and inspiring them to take action.

This chapter is your compass, pointing you in a new direction. It's about understanding your role in the affiliate marketing ecosystem. You're not just a link or a salesperson; you're a storyteller, a guide, a trusted source. You have the potential to change lives and create a legacy.

As you embark on this journey, remember that your actions aren't confined to a computer screen or smartphone. They ripple through the lives of those you touch. Your content, your recommendations, your insights have the power to influence decisions, shape choices, and lead to transformations.

It's time to embrace affiliate marketing with a renewed sense of purpose and passion. It's not just a profession; it's a mission. It's not just a source of income; it's a source of inspiration. You're not just a marketer; you're an influencer, a guide, a trailblazer.

Affiliate marketing redefined starts here. Will you join us on this extraordinary journey? Will you be the change the digital world has been waiting for? The path is yours to take, and we're here to light the way. Let's get started!

CHAPTER TWO

The Affiliate Marketing Essentials

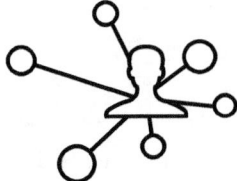

Welcome to Chapter 2, where we dive deep into the core of affiliate marketing and set the stage for your journey. It's not just about mastering the basics; it's about harnessing your potential and charting your course for success.

Imagine affiliate marketing as a vast ocean, and you're about to set sail. In this chapter, you'll learn how to choose your destination, navigate the waters, and ultimately reach your goals. But it all begins with your choices.

Choosing Your Niche: Don't Follow, Lead

Affiliate marketing isn't just about promoting products; it's about sharing your passion, expertise, and interests with the world. Don't simply follow trends or popular niches. Instead, lead with your genuine enthusiasm.

Your niche is your playground, your canvas, and your realm of expertise. It's where your authenticity shines. So, explore your interests, find what truly captivates you, and turn that passion into a niche. When you're genuinely excited about what you're marketing, your audience will notice.

Researching Your Audience: Who Are You Serving?

Successful affiliate marketing isn't a one-way street; it's a conversation. Your audience is your partner on this journey, so get to know them intimately. Dive deep into their needs, desires, and pain points. What keeps them awake at night, and how can you provide solutions?

Your audience is not a faceless crowd; they are real people with real concerns. Connect with them, engage with them, and build trust. When you understand their world, you can offer real value.

Goal Setting: Charting Your Course

Affiliate marketing isn't a blind journey; it's a well-planned expedition. What do you want to achieve? Set clear, tangible goals. Whether it's a specific income target, the number of leads, or creating valuable content, establish your objectives.

Goals act as your compass. They keep you on track and focused. They transform dreams into actionable steps. Don't just set them; commit to them.

Joining the Right Affiliate Programs

Not all affiliate programs are created equal. In this chapter, you'll learn how to select programs that align with your niche, your audience, and your values. Don't settle for the first program that comes your way; choose partners that share your vision.

Building a Strong Online Presence: Beyond the Basics

Your online presence is your digital home, your sanctuary. In this chapter, we'll explore how to create an engaging website, design a compelling platform, and establish a commanding presence. Your online space is where you showcase your expertise and engage with your audience.

Affiliate marketing is more than just transactions; it's about transformation. It's about making a meaningful connection and leaving an impact. By making the right choices and charting your course, you'll transform the affiliate marketing landscape and set a course for success.

Your journey begins with these fundamentals, but it's your choices, your authenticity, and your dedication that will lead you to new horizons. So, are you ready to embrace your niche, connect with your audience, set your goals, choose your partners, and build your digital presence? The voyage is yours to take, and we're here to navigate it together. Let's set sail!

CHAPTER THREE

Content Creation Unleashed

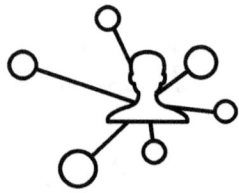

Welcome to the powerhouse of your affiliate marketing journey – Chapter 3! Here, we unleash the full potential of your content creation abilities. It's not just about writing words; it's about crafting stories, shaping perceptions, and driving change. Are you ready to tap into the creative force within you? Let's dive in.

Quality Over Quantity: Mastering Content Creation

In this digital era, content is king, and your role as an affiliate marketer is to wear the crown with pride. But remember, it's not about churning out endless streams of content. Quality reigns supreme. Your content should educate, inspire, and engage. It should be a source of value.

Your articles, videos, and social media posts are not just words on a screen; they're your tools for building trust and making connections. Your audience is looking for content that speaks to them personally, content that resonates with their experiences and addresses their questions.

SEO Simplified: A Straightforward Approach

Search Engine Optimization (SEO) can seem like a labyrinth, but we're here to simplify it. Think of SEO as your treasure map. It guides your audience to your content. But remember, the real treasure is your knowledge, your insights, and your solutions

Keywords are your markers on the map. But don't just stuff your content with keywords. Use them naturally, like breadcrumbs leading your audience on a journey. Craft content that ranks high on search engines, not by tricks, but through value.

Crafting Engaging Content

Your content is your vessel; it should carry your audience on a journey. It should captivate their attention and never let go. Engaging content makes your audience stay, return, and share. It's content that sparks discussions and inspires actions.

So, think beyond the ordinary. Use engaging headlines, vivid visuals, and compelling narratives. Share personal anecdotes, real-life examples, and emotional triggers. Make your audience not just readers but participants in your story.

The Power of Storytelling: Beyond Information

Don't just provide information; tell stories. Stories are how we connect, how we remember, and how we're moved to action. They're the bridges that lead from your world to your audience's

We'll explore the art of storytelling, the structure of a compelling story, and the emotional pull it creates. Your affiliate marketing journey is not just about facts and figures; it's about the stories you weave.

Your content is your chance to inspire, educate, and entertain. It's your canvas for creativity and your platform for sharing your wisdom. Are you ready to create content that not only informs but transforms? Get ready to unleash the creative force within and shape your narrative in the affiliate marketing world. The spotlight is on you, and the stage is set. Let's create content that changes lives and sparks action!

CHAPTER FOUR

Affiliate Programs Demystified

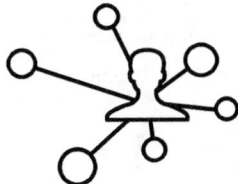

Chapter 4 is here, and it's all about demystifying the world of affiliate programs. We'll unravel the secrets, explore the opportunities, and empower you with the knowledge to make informed choices. It's not just about joining programs; it's about becoming a discerning affiliate marketer who sets their own course.

Cracking the Code of Affiliate Programs

Affiliate programs can seem like enigmatic doors into the digital world. But in our club, we hand you the key. These programs are your gateways to the products and services you'll promote. Your choice of programs is pivotal

Consider your niche, your audience, and your goals when selecting affiliate programs. Don't just go for the most popular; choose those that align with your values and resonate with your audience. Remember, you're not just an affiliate; you're a curator of solutions.

The Key Affiliate Networks

Affiliate networks are like bustling marketplaces. They connect affiliates (like you) with merchants offering products or services. They are the heart of affiliate marketing, where transactions happen.

We'll dive into the top affiliate networks and show you how to navigate them effectively. It's not about just signing up; it's about building relationships, understanding the marketplace, and making the right choices.

Selection Criteria: Separating the Best from the Rest

Not all affiliate programs are created equal. Some will offer you riches, while others will leave you empty-handed. How do you tell the difference? We've got you covered.

We'll discuss the selection criteria that set the best affiliate programs apart. Look for fair commissions, reliable tracking systems, and a history of on-time payments. Seek programs that offer valuable resources, promotional materials, and affiliate support. It's not just about what they offer but how they support you in your journey.

Navigating Affiliate Program Terms

In affiliate marketing, you'll encounter terms and conditions that can be like fine print in a contract. But we'll make sure you not only read but understand the fine print. This is not just about signing up; it's about compliance and transparency.

We'll explore the terms and conditions that you should be aware of. From disclosure requirements to promotional restrictions, you'll be equipped to navigate affiliate agreements confidently.

Affiliate programs are not just contracts; they're partnerships. They're your ticket to a world of opportunities, but it's essential to choose wisely. The choices you make here will define your path as an affiliate marketer.

As we proceed, remember that this journey is about more than transactions; it's about transformations. Affiliate programs are not just about joining; they're about building relationships and finding partners who share your values. Your role is not just to promote products; it's to curate solutions and guide your audience.

So, are you ready to demystify affiliate programs and choose your partners with wisdom? It's not just about joining; it's about becoming an affiliate marketer who sets their own standards and shapes the digital landscape. The journey continues, and the spotlight is on you. Let's unlock the doors to your affiliate marketing future!

CHAPTER FIVE

Promotion Reimagined

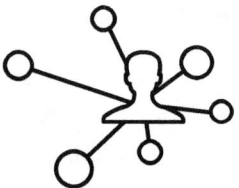

Welcome to Chapter 5, where we take a fresh perspective on promotion. It's not just about marketing; it's about making an impact. Your approach to promotion can be a game-changer, not just for your affiliate marketing journey, but for the lives of your audience. Let's dive in and explore the art of promotion reimagined.

Beyond Conventional Promotion

Conventional promotion often involves pushing products, shouting discounts, and bombarding your audience with sales pitches. But we're here to challenge the status quo. Promotion should be about connecting, not just convincing.

In our club, we promote by educating, engaging, and inspiring. We aim to offer solutions, not just products. Your role is not just to sell; it's to guide, to inform, and to build trust. When you approach promotion with this mindset, you become more than a marketer; you become a trusted advisor.

Email Marketing Secrets: Building Connections

Email marketing is a powerful tool, but it's not about spamming inboxes with generic messages. It's about building connections, nurturing relationships, and offering value.

We'll explore the art of crafting compelling emails, segmenting your audience, and delivering content that resonates. Your emails should be a welcome sight in your subscribers' inboxes, not an annoyance. Build connections, and your audience will reward you with trust and loyalty.

Social Media Unleashed: A New Perspective

Social media is not just a platform; it's a community. It's not about broadcasting; it's about engaging. When you approach social media with authenticity, it can become a powerful tool for building relationships and expanding your reach

We'll delve into the strategies for effective social media marketing. It's about more than likes and shares; it's about meaningful interactions and genuine connections.

Paid Advertising Made Simple

Paid advertising can be intimidating, but it's also a way to amplify your message and reach a wider audience. When used wisely, it's not just about spending money; it's about investing in your brand.

We'll discuss how to create compelling ad campaigns that resonate with your audience, as well as budgeting and monitoring your ads. Paid advertising is not about emptying your pockets; it's about strategic investments that yield returns.

Webinars and Live Streaming: Connect, Convert, Conquer

Webinars and live streaming are like a bridge between you and your audience. They allow for real-time interactions, questions, and genuine connections.

We'll explore how to create engaging webinars and live streams that connect, convert, and conquer. It's not just about presenting; it's about engaging and inspiring your audience in real-time.

SEO Revisited: Optimization for Results

Search Engine Optimization (SEO) is not just about keywords; it's about optimizing your content for human readers. It's about providing valuable, relevant content that resonates.

We'll revisit SEO with a focus on optimization for results. It's not about gaming search engines; it's about ranking high by providing value to your audience.

The Influencer Advantage: A Unique Approach

Influencer marketing can be a game-changer in your affiliate marketing journey. We'll explore how to collaborate with influencers in a way that benefits both parties and provides value to your audience.

It's not about just partnering with influencers; it's about forming meaningful collaborations that extend your reach and offer your audience unique perspectives.

Promotion is not just about pushing products; it's about making an impact. Your approach to promotion should inspire, inform, and engage your audience. It's not just about selling; it's about building trust and offering solutions.

So, are you ready to reimagine your approach to promotion? It's not just about marketing; it's about connecting and making a lasting impact. Your promotion can be a force for positive change. Let's dive into the art of promotion reimagined and inspire your audience along the way!

CHAPTER SIX

Crafting Quality Content

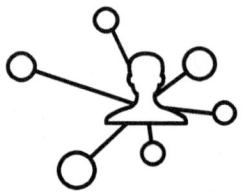

Welcome to Chapter 6, where we're going to unleash the true potential of your content creation. Quality content isn't just an option; it's the driving force behind your success as an affiliate marketer. This is the chapter where we explore the art of crafting content that captivates, resonates, and transforms.

Unveiling High-Quality Content

Quality content is the heart and soul of your affiliate marketing journey. It's not just about words on a page; it's about creating an experience.

Your content should be a journey for your audience, an exploration of knowledge, and an opportunity for transformation.

High-quality content isn't just informative; it's engaging, inspiring, and solution-oriented. It's the kind of content that keeps your audience coming back for more. It's not just about quantity; it's about depth and impact.

SEO Best Practices for Real Results

Search Engine Optimization (SEO) isn't a magic formula for success, but it's a powerful tool when used wisely. It's about creating content that ranks high on search engines not by trickery but by providing genuine value.

We'll explore SEO best practices that guide your content optimization. Your content should be designed for both search engines and human readers. It's not about stuffing keywords; it's about enhancing your content's reach by addressing your audience's needs.

Content Types That Connect

Your content isn't one-size-fits-all. Different types of content cater to different preferences and learning styles. In this chapter, we'll explore a range of content types and how to choose the ones that best resonate with your audience.

Whether it's blog posts, videos, infographics, or podcasts, each content type has its strengths. By diversifying your content, you can engage a broader audience and offer value in various ways.

The Art of Captivating Headlines and Hooks

The first thing your audience sees is your headline, and it can make or break their decision to engage with your content. Your headline should be a doorway into your world, an invitation to explore.

We'll discuss the art of crafting captivating headlines and hooks that draw readers in. It's not about clickbait; it's about creating intrigue and setting expectations for your content.

Storytelling: Your Secret Weapon

Storytelling isn't just for novels and movies; it's a powerful tool in content creation. Stories are how we connect, how we remember, and how we're inspired to take action.

In this chapter, we'll explore the art of storytelling. Your content should not be a dry recitation of facts but a narrative that engages, informs, and inspires. Stories are the bridges that connect your content to your audience's experiences.

Visual Content That Speaks Volumes

Visual content is a potent means of engaging your audience. It's not just about images; it's about creating visuals that enhance your message and resonate with your audience.

We'll dive into the world of visual content, from images and infographics to videos and interactive media. Your visuals should complement and enhance your content, providing a richer experience for your audience.

Mobile Optimization: A Must, Not an Option

In today's digital world, mobile optimization is not an option; it's a necessity. Your content should be accessible and engaging for mobile users. We'll explore the strategies for optimizing your content for mobile devices.

Your content should adapt seamlessly to various screen sizes and load quickly on mobile devices. Mobile optimization is about providing a smooth, enjoyable experience for your on-the-go audience.

Proofreading and Perfection

Quality content isn't just about the message; it's about the presentation. Your content should be free from errors, both grammatical and factual. Proofreading is your final polish.

We'll discuss the importance of proofreading and how to ensure your content is error-free. A well-polished piece of content not only shows professionalism but also enhances your message's impact.

Your content isn't just information; it's an experience. It's the journey you take your audience on, the stories you tell, and the solutions you provide. In the world of affiliate marketing, high-quality content is your secret weapon, your ticket to building trust, and your tool for making an impact.

So, are you ready to craft quality content that captivates, resonates, and transforms? It's not just about writing; it's about creating experiences. Let's dive into the art of content creation and elevate your affiliate marketing journey to new heights!

CHAPTER SEVEN

Tracking Your Success

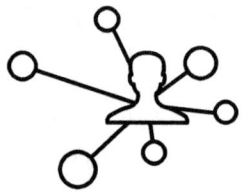

Welcome to Chapter 7, where we dive into the fascinating world of tracking and analytics. This isn't just about numbers and charts; it's about gaining insights, measuring your progress, and making informed decisions. Tracking your success is more than a routine; it's your compass to navigate the digital landscape and reach new heights.

Setting the Stage for Success

Before you can measure your success, you need to define it. In this chapter, we'll discuss the importance of setting clear, measurable goals for your affiliate marketing journey. Your goals are your beacons of light, guiding you through the sometimes foggy waters of the digital realm.

Your goals should be specific, measurable, attainable, relevant, and time-bound (SMART). When you have well-defined goals, tracking your progress becomes more straightforward. You'll know what to focus on, and your efforts will become more purposeful.

Tracking Conversions: Measuring Impact

Conversions are the lifeblood of affiliate marketing. Whether it's a sale, a lead, or any other predefined action, conversions indicate that your efforts are paying off. We'll explore how to track conversions accurately and why they matter.

Conversion tracking tools can provide invaluable data about your audience's behavior. By understanding how your audience interacts with your content, you can tailor your approach to increase conversions.

Key Metrics to Watch

In the world of affiliate marketing, metrics are your allies. We'll discuss essential metrics that you should monitor regularly. These include click-through rates (CTR), conversion rates, traffic sources, and more. Each metric provides a piece of the puzzle, helping you understand what's working and what needs improvement.

Remember that it's not just about collecting data; it's about using that data to refine your strategies. Metrics are your compass, showing you the way forward.

Google Analytics Unveiled

Google Analytics is a powerful tool that provides a wealth of information about your website's performance. We'll delve into how to set up and use Google Analytics to track your success. This free tool can give you insights into visitor demographics, behavior, and more.

The data you gather from Google Analytics can help you make informed decisions. You'll learn which content resonates most with your audience and where your traffic is coming from. This knowledge can guide your content creation and promotional strategies.

A/B Testing: The Path to Perfection

A/B testing is a methodology that allows you to compare two versions of a webpage or piece of content to see which one performs better. We'll discuss how to use A/B testing to optimize your content and maximize conversions.

By continuously testing different elements, such as headlines, visuals, and calls to action, you can fine-tune your content for the best results. A/B testing is about constant improvement, not settling for the status quo.

Leveraging Affiliate Dashboards

Affiliate programs often provide dashboards that offer insights into your performance as an affiliate marketer. We'll explore how to make the most of these dashboards, interpret the data they provide, and use it to your advantage.

Affiliate dashboards can help you track your commissions, monitor your referrals, and gain a deep understanding of how your efforts are paying off. Use these tools to identify what's working and what needs adjustment.

Regular Analysis and Adaptation

Tracking and analytics aren't a one-time effort; they're ongoing. We'll discuss the importance of regularly analyzing your data and adapting your strategies. The digital landscape is constantly changing, and your affiliate marketing journey should be dynamic, too.

By analyzing your data and staying updated on industry trends, you can make data-driven decisions and stay ahead of the curve. It's not just about tracking; it's about adapting and evolving.

Your affiliate marketing journey is a dynamic, ever-changing adventure. Tracking your success isn't just about numbers; it's about understanding your audience, fine-tuning your strategies, and navigating the digital landscape effectively.

So, are you ready to set clear goals, track your conversions, monitor key metrics, and use tools like Google Analytics and A/B testing to your advantage? Your success as an affiliate marketer depends on your ability to measure and adapt. Let's dive into the world of tracking and analytics and unlock your potential for greatness!

CHAPTER EIGHT

Compliance and Legal Considerations

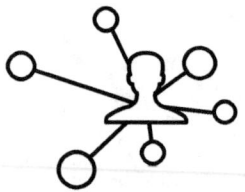

Welcome to Chapter 8, where we explore an often overlooked but crucial aspect of affiliate marketing—compliance and legal considerations. This isn't just about rules and regulations; it's about building trust, protecting your brand, and ensuring that you're on the right side of the law. Let's navigate this essential terrain.

Ethics in Affiliate Marketing

Before we delve into the legal aspects, let's talk about ethics. Affiliate marketing is built on trust. Your audience trusts your recommendations, and this trust is fragile. Unethical practices can quickly erode this trust.

We'll discuss the importance of ethical affiliate marketing. It's not just about making sales; it's about providing genuine value. Be transparent, honest, and disclose your affiliate relationships clearly. Your audience deserves this respect.

FTC Guidelines: Your North Star

The Federal Trade Commission (FTC) has guidelines that govern affiliate marketing practices in the United States. We'll explore these guidelines and what they mean for your affiliate marketing journey. Even if you're not based in the U.S., these guidelines provide a valuable framework for ethical marketing.

Disclosure is the key. The FTC guidelines emphasize transparency, ensuring that your audience knows when you're promoting affiliate products. We'll discuss how to make these disclosures clear and prominent.

EU GDPR and Data Protection

If you operate within the European Union or handle data from EU residents, you must be aware of the General Data Protection Regulation (GDPR). This regulation sets strict standards for data protection and user privacy.

We'll explore the key principles of GDPR, such as obtaining clear consent, respecting users' rights, and ensuring data security. Understanding and complying with GDPR is not just about avoiding fines; it's about respecting your audience's privacy and building trust.

CAN-SPAM Act: Email Marketing Regulations

If you engage in email marketing, you must be familiar with the Controlling the Assault of Non-Solicited Pornography And Marketing (CAN-SPAM) Act. This act outlines rules for commercial email, and we'll discuss how it impacts your affiliate marketing efforts.

From providing clear opt-out options to including your physical address, complying with CAN-SPAM is about respecting your audience's inbox. Remember, email marketing should be about building connections, not annoying your subscribers.

International Regulations: A Global Perspective

Affiliate marketing is a global endeavor, and regulations vary from country to country. We'll provide an overview of some international regulations that may affect your affiliate marketing efforts.

Whether it's the Canadian Anti-Spam Legislation (CASL) or the Australian Spam Act, understanding and respecting these regulations is not just about compliance; it's about respecting the diverse audiences you serve.

Protecting Your Brand and Reputation

Legal compliance isn't just about following rules; it's about safeguarding your brand and reputation. Ethical, lawful practices are your armor in the digital world. Building a trustworthy brand is an ongoing effort that hinges on your commitment to compliance and ethics.

Your audience is your greatest asset. Treat them with respect, protect their data, and be transparent about your affiliate relationships. These actions will not only keep you on the right side of the law but also cement your reputation as an affiliate marketer of integrity.

Compliance and legal considerations might not be the most exciting aspects of affiliate marketing, but they are the pillars of trust and credibility. It's not just about following rules; it's about respecting your audience, protecting your brand, and navigating the digital landscape with integrity.

Are you ready to embrace ethical affiliate marketing, follow FTC guidelines, respect data privacy regulations, and safeguard your brand's reputation? Compliance isn't a burden; it's a badge of honor that sets you apart in the affiliate marketing world. Let's dive into the world of compliance and legal considerations and become trusted ambassadors in the digital realm!

CHAPTER NINE

Scaling Your Affiliate Marketing Business

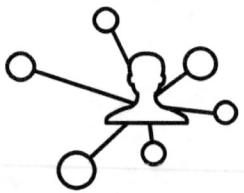

Welcome to Chapter 9, where we'll explore the exhilarating journey of scaling your affiliate marketing business. This chapter isn't just about growth; it's about taking your efforts to the next level, expanding your reach, and achieving remarkable results. Are you ready to elevate your affiliate marketing game? Let's get started.

The Mindset of Growth

Scaling your affiliate marketing business starts with a growth mindset. It's about thinking beyond the status quo and setting your sights on bigger horizons. As you navigate the digital landscape, remember that your potential for growth is boundless.

Believe in your ability to expand your influence and serve a wider audience. It's not just about the size of your business; it's about the impact you can make. Embrace challenges and view them as opportunities for growth.

Diversifying Your Income Streams

Relying on a single income source can be risky in the ever-evolving world of affiliate marketing. We'll discuss the importance of diversifying your income streams. By promoting a variety of products and services within your niche, you can protect your business against unexpected shifts in the market.

Diversification isn't just about safeguarding your income; it's about offering more value to your audience. When you can cater to various needs, your audience becomes more engaged and your business more resilient.

Building a Team: The Power of Delegation

As your affiliate marketing business grows, so do your responsibilities. Delegating tasks is a crucial step in scaling your business. We'll explore how to build and manage a team, whether it's virtual assistants, content creators, or marketing specialists.

Delegation is not about letting go of control; it's about focusing your efforts on strategic decisions and high-impact tasks. With a capable team, you can expand your reach and provide more value to your audience.

Leveraging Automation

Automation is your ally in efficiency. We'll delve into how to automate routine tasks, such as email marketing, social media posting, and analytics tracking. Automation frees up your time, allowing you to focus on higher-value activities.

Your time is your most precious resource; use it wisely. By automating repetitive tasks, you can scale your efforts without working around the clock.

Expanding Your Promotional Strategies

Scaling your affiliate marketing business involves exploring new promotional strategies. We'll discuss advanced techniques like influencer marketing, joint ventures, and paid advertising campaigns.

These strategies open up new avenues for reaching a broader audience. Remember, it's not just about increasing the quantity of your promotions; it's about enhancing the quality and impact of your marketing efforts.

Mastering Customer Relationship Management (CRM)

Effective customer relationship management is vital for scaling your business. We'll explore how to manage and nurture your relationships with your audience, turning one-time customers into loyal fans.

A well-implemented CRM strategy is not just about sales; it's about understanding your audience's needs, providing personalized solutions, and building lasting connections.

Continuous Learning and Adaptation

Scaling your affiliate marketing business isn't a one-time achievement; it's an ongoing journey. Stay committed to continuous learning and adaptation. Embrace new technologies, trends, and strategies to remain at the forefront of your niche.

Your ability to adapt and stay ahead of the curve is what will propel your business to new heights. It's not just about growth; it's about sustainable, long-term success.

Are you ready to embrace a growth mindset, diversify your income streams, build a capable team, leverage automation, and explore advanced promotional strategies? Scaling your affiliate marketing business is an adventure of endless possibilities. Let's embark on this journey of expansion, impact, and remarkable results!

CHAPTER TEN

Common Affiliate Marketing Mistakes to Avoid

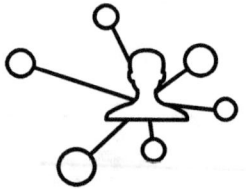

Welcome to Chapter 10, where we'll shine a spotlight on the common affiliate marketing mistakes that can be your roadblocks to success. Knowing these pitfalls is the first step to avoiding them. It's not just about sidestepping errors; it's about setting yourself up for an unobstructed path to success. Let's dive in and learn from the missteps of others.

1. Neglecting Your Audience

One of the most significant mistakes in affiliate marketing is neglecting your audience's needs. Your audience is your compass, guiding you toward valuable content and products. Failing to understand their desires and problems can lead to disconnected marketing efforts.

Instead, actively engage with your audience. Listen to their feedback, ask for their opinions, and tailor your content to address their specific needs. Your audience is the heartbeat of your affiliate marketing journey; listen closely.

2. Promoting Everything Under the Sun

While it might be tempting to promote every product or service under the sun, this scattergun approach can dilute your message and overwhelm your audience. Promoting too many products can lead to a lack of focus and trust issues.

Instead, focus on a select few products or services that align with your niche and audience's interests. Quality beats quantity. By promoting only what genuinely benefits your audience, you'll build trust and authority.

3. Ignoring Product Quality

Promoting a low-quality product for the sake of a quick commission is a mistake many affiliate marketers make. This can damage your reputation and erode trust with your audience.

Before promoting any product, ensure its quality and relevance to your audience. Your audience's trust is your most valuable asset; don't compromise it for short-term gains.

4. Overlooking Transparency and Disclosure

Failing to disclose your affiliate relationships is a grave error. It erodes trust and can lead to legal consequences. The FTC and other regulatory bodies require clear disclosures in affiliate marketing.

Be transparent about your affiliate relationships in a prominent and easily understandable way. Honesty builds trust, and trust is the foundation of successful affiliate marketing.

5. Neglecting Mobile Optimization*

In today's mobile-first world, neglecting mobile optimization is a significant mistake. If your content and website aren't mobile-friendly, you're missing out on a vast audience.

Optimize your content, website, and emails for mobile devices. Mobile optimization is not just about staying relevant; it's about providing a smooth, user-friendly experience.

6. Skipping A/B Testing

A/B testing is a powerful tool for optimizing your marketing efforts, but many affiliate marketers overlook it. Failing to test different approaches can mean missed opportunities for improvement.

Embrace A/B testing to fine-tune your strategies and enhance your results. It's not just about getting things right the first time; it's about ongoing improvement.

7. Neglecting Data Analysis

Data is a goldmine of insights, but neglecting data analysis is a grave mistake. Without analyzing your metrics and performance, you're operating in the dark.

Regularly analyze your data to make informed decisions and adapt your strategies. Data is your compass, guiding you toward your goals.

8. Falling for Get-Rich-Quick Schemes

Affiliate marketing is not a get-rich-quick scheme. Falling for such promises can lead to disappointment and wasted resources. Success in affiliate marketing takes time and effort.

Be wary of schemes that promise instant wealth. Instead, focus on building a sustainable, long-term business that provides genuine value.

9. Resisting Change and Adaptation

The digital landscape is ever-evolving, and resisting change and adaptation is a significant mistake. Stagnation can lead to obsolescence.

Embrace change and stay up-to-date with industry trends. Your ability to adapt is what will set you apart in the fast-paced world of affiliate marketing.

10. Losing Patience and Persistence

Success in affiliate marketing requires patience and persistence. Impatience and giving up too soon are common mistakes that can hinder your progress.

Remember that success is a journey, not a destination. Stay persistent, keep learning, and stay the course. Great achievements take time.

Learning from these common mistakes is your roadmap to success. It's not just about avoiding pitfalls; it's about building a sturdy foundation for your affiliate marketing journey. Embrace these lessons, and let them guide you toward a brighter and more successful future.

CHAPTER ELEVEN

Success Stories and Inspirations

Welcome to Chapter 11, where we're going to dive into a treasure trove of success stories and inspirations. Learning from those who've walked the affiliate marketing path before you can be a powerful motivator. These stories aren't just about what's possible; they're about what's possible for you. Let's explore the journeys of individuals who turned dreams into reality and discover how you can do the same.

The Power of Resilience

Success stories are often tales of resilience. They remind us that setbacks are not roadblocks; they are stepping stones. Consider the story of

Jackie, who faced numerous rejections before finally finding the perfect product to promote. Her journey wasn't a straight line to success, but it was marked by determination and unwavering belief in her abilities.

From Side Hustle to Full-Time Success

Many affiliate marketers start as side hustlers, balancing their marketing efforts with other responsibilities. These stories remind us that success doesn't always require an immediate leap into full-time entrepreneurship. Jackie began her affiliate marketing journey while holding down a full-time nursing job. Through dedication and a well-thought-out strategy, she eventually transitioned into full-time affiliate marketing, turning her side hustle into a thriving business.

The Impact of Niche Passion

Passion is a driving force behind many affiliate marketers' success. Jackie chose a niche she was deeply passionate about, allowing her to create authentic content and connect with her audience on a profound level. Her story serves as a reminder that when you love what you do, your enthusiasm shines through in your marketing efforts.

Taking Advantage of Training and Mentorship

Success often comes quicker when you have the right guidance. Jackie didn't hesitate to seek training and mentorship from experienced affiliate marketers. Her journey is a testament to the power of learning from those who've already paved the way. It's a reminder that success leaves clues, and seeking guidance can significantly accelerate your progress.

Community and Collaboration

Affiliate marketing isn't a solo journey for everyone. Jackie found success by collaborating with others and tapping into the power of community. Their story underscores the importance of networking, partnerships, and learning from fellow marketers. It's a testament to the strength of the affiliate marketing community.

The Global Reach of Affiliate Marketing

Affiliate marketing knows no geographical boundaries. Jackie discovered success by embracing a global audience. Her journey is a reminder that the digital world offers a vast marketplace, and with the right strategies, you can reach audiences around the world. The success of affiliate marketing is not limited by borders.

Creating a Legacy

Affiliate marketing can be a path to not only financial success but also leaving a lasting legacy. Jackie built a brand that's not only profitable but also makes a positive impact in her niche. Her story serves as an inspiration for those who want to leave a mark and create something bigger than themselves.

These success stories are not just about celebrating the achievements of others; they're about realizing your potential. Affiliate marketing is not reserved for a select few; it's a journey that anyone can embark on. These stories show that the road to success may have twists and turns, but with determination, passion, and the right strategies, you can achieve remarkable results.

So, are you ready to be inspired by the journeys of those who've walked the affiliate marketing path before you? These success stories are not just about what's possible for them; they're about what's possible for you. Let's draw motivation from these inspiring tales and embark on our own affiliate marketing adventures!

CHAPTER TWELVE

Conclusion and Next Steps

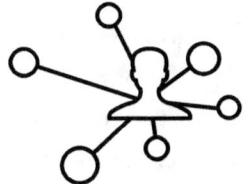

Congratulations on reaching the final chapter of this incredible journey. You've now traveled through the world of affiliate marketing, from its foundations to the heights of success. This chapter is not just about closing the book; it's about opening doors to your future. Let's conclude this guide with a sense of achievement, clarity, and a roadmap for what lies ahead.

Reflecting on Your Journey

Take a moment to reflect on how far you've come. You've gained a deep understanding of affiliate marketing, learned strategies and techniques, and explored the stories of those who've succeeded. Remember, learning is not a destination; it's a lifelong journey. Celebrate your progress and recognize that this is just the beginning.

Your Unique Affiliate Marketing Path

Your affiliate marketing journey is unique, and it's about finding your path within this dynamic world. Don't compare yourself to others; focus on your goals, your audience, and your passion. You have your unique story to tell, and your journey will unfold uniquely.

A Commitment to Excellence

Excellence in affiliate marketing is not a one-time achievement; it's a commitment. It's about consistently delivering value to your audience, continuously learning, and adapting to changes in the digital landscape. Success in this field is an ongoing adventure, and you have the power to achieve greatness.

Next Steps for Your Success

The conclusion of one journey is the beginning of another. As you close this chapter, it's essential to define your next steps. Here's a roadmap for your affiliate marketing success:

1. **Set Clear Goals:** Define your short-term and long-term goals. What do you want to achieve in the next month, year, or five years? Your goals will guide your efforts.

2. **Create an Action Plan:** Develop a detailed action plan that outlines the steps you'll take to reach your goals. What strategies will you implement, and how will you measure success?

3. **Continuous Learning:** Commit to ongoing learning. Stay updated on industry trends, marketing techniques, and new technologies. The digital landscape evolves rapidly, and your knowledge should, too

4. **Networking:** Connect with fellow affiliate marketers and professionals in your niche. Networking can open doors to collaborations, partnerships, and mentorship.

5. **Content Creation:** Continue to create high-quality content that resonates with your audience. Consistency is key; regular content creation builds trust and authority.

6. **Monitoring and Analysis:** Regularly track your performance using analytics tools. Data-driven decisions are the cornerstone of success.

7. **Scaling and Diversification:** As you gain experience, consider scaling your efforts and diversifying your income streams. Explore new niches, products, or strategies.

8. **Community Building:** Nurture your audience and create a strong community. Your audience is your greatest asset; treat them with respect and appreciation.

Your Affiliate Marketing Legacy

Affiliate marketing is not just about making money; it's about creating a legacy. Your journey can leave a positive impact on your audience, your niche, and the digital marketing world. Your legacy is a testament to your commitment to excellence, ethics, and genuine value.

As you close this chapter and embark on the next phase of your affiliate marketing journey, remember that success is a journey, not a destination. Your path will have challenges, but with dedication, resilience, and a commitment to excellence, you have the power to achieve remarkable results.

So, are you ready to embrace your unique affiliate marketing path, set clear goals, and commit to ongoing excellence? Your journey is yours to shape, and the possibilities are endless. Let's conclude this chapter with a sense of accomplishment and a burning enthusiasm for what's to come. Your affiliate marketing adventure continues, and your future is full of potential!

"The Only Time is Now"

You've made it to the end of this incredible journey, and I applaud your commitment to learning, growing, and making your mark in the world of affiliate marketing. But remember, the end of one chapter is the beginning of another. Your journey towards success and financial freedom doesn't stop here; it's only just beginning.

I'm thrilled to introduce you to our next empowering resource, "The Now-or-Never Wealth Blueprint." This book takes all the principles and strategies you've learned in this guide and dives even deeper, providing you with a step-by-step roadmap to turn your dreams into reality. It's not just about what to do; it's about how to do it.

In "The Now-or-Never Wealth Blueprint," you'll find all the insider secrets that gurus often hide behind expensive courses. We've compiled the most valuable resources, links, and tips that are worth their weight in gold. What's more, we've made it accessible to you without the sky-high price tags that many competitors charge.

This book is your key to unlocking the next level of your affiliate marketing journey. It's your guide to turning your passion into profit, scaling your income, and achieving the financial freedom you've always desired.

So don't wait; seize the opportunity now. Click on the link below to get your hands on "The Now-or-Never Wealth Blueprint" and take the next giant leap towards your dreams. Your success story is waiting to be written, and this book is your pen and paper.

[Click here to purchase "The Now-or-Never Wealth Blueprint"]

https://stan.store/eklektikdigital

Don't miss out on this game-changing resource. Your journey to financial freedom and success is now in your hands. Get your copy today, and let's continue this incredible adventure together. Your dreams are worth it!